Angelic Sinner

Kylie Archer

BookLeaf Publishing

Presentation by *BookLeaf Publishing*

Web: www.bookleafpub.com

E-mail: info@bookleafpub.com

ISBN: 9789357441391

First edition 2023

This book is dedicated to all the lost and lonely souls. There is a place for you. Don't give up on yourself or your dreams.

ACKNOWLEDGEMENT

I give my thanks to the Lord above me of course, the universe, my fellow empaths and poets. I also give deep thanks to my grandma and my mama who always told me I was a good writer. To my soul sister Crystal whom always inspires me and My English teacher Mrs Robert's who did more for me than she'll ever know. Thank you for seeing me.

PREFACE

I will take you on a journey that has twists and turns, beauty and edge. These are my thoughts laid out across these pages. You will feel what I have felt and maybe be a little different inside. If I were to inspire just one person; that would be enough. Because one person can change the world

A Talk With My Heart

I had a talk with my heart
And it told me no
It has all the power
What it says goes
I've tried to stop it
But it doesn't listen
It does what it wants
And does what it pleases
It causes me great pain
Let's me crash and fall
Drives me insane
I wish i was in control
But this heart of mine
Always seems to leave
a gaping hole

Rare

Her lips are like nothing else
So unnatural when she talks
She'll put you under a spell
And have you on dead lock
And when you taste her kiss
You'll be hypnotized
The amount of bliss
That you've ever fantasized
Her eyes are so rare
So beautifuly green
You can't help but stare
Like pure ecstasy
She'll look at you and study
Do not be afraid
She's seeing into you
With her you are safe
She will see what you bring
And what you don't say
If you are ready
Then you will remain
Her touch is like heroin
Such a powerful drug
Even though it makes you weak
You can't get enough
Her body will linger

On your skin
You will be in awe
And wonder where she's been
She is beauty at its finest
But don't take her for granted
Because she'll be this sweet
And use it to her advantage

Will You?

Will you still love me
If I show you my darkness
It gets real cold there
Colder than the Arctic
Just bear with me baby
Love my broken parts
I don't need you to heal me
Just protect my broken heart
Will you still want me?
After my deepest of low
Sorry if I'm a type of way
Sometimes here it'll snow
Just hold on my love
And I promise you
I will pick myself up
I will break through
Just don't give up on me
Thats the last thing I need
Will you still love me
After I show you my scars
All alone in the corner
Sitting here in the dark
Will you still see me
the same way
After I show you
Every ounce of my pain

Spiraling

I am slowly losing it
I can feel it deep inside
I am becoming detached
Drifting far from my mind
These emotions I've supressed
For quite some time
Are slowly being expressed
But surely forming a line
I'm coming undone
Unraveling the threads
One by one
So fucked in the head
Gonna completely break
No more pretending
For fucks sake
I cant keep on bending
So fucking lost
So fucking broke
So fucking done
I have reached my breaking point
I am losing myself
They will soon all see
Gonna completely shut down
No more Kylie
Just an empty memory...

Constant Battle

Ups and downs
Highs and lows
Over thinking
Wanting to know
Happy and sorrow
Smiles and tears
Racing thoughts
Racing fears
Complete and empty
Giggles and screams
A constant war
Ripping seams
Lost and found
Here and there
Cannot breathe
This toxic air
Whole and apart
Together and broken
So many words
Left unspoken
Close and far
Simple and complex
A mind fuck
From life's tests
Brave and afraid

Weak and strong
A constant wonder
Where I belong
A constant battle
Between right and wrong
A constant struggle
To go along
The master
The slave
In a world so bright
Full of gray...

PTSD

Fireworks
I used to love them
But now I dread when they come
My whole body jumps
And my heart beat now thumps
Even if I'm prepared
I still get scared
I miss being able to relax
But ever since I left
My minds under attack
I used to think
You were the fireworks
In my sky
Didnt realize I was so blind
To all your lies
I hate to admit it but,
I think you took my 4th of July

It wouldn't Be Fair

You ask me what's on my mind
And I look at you and ask why
You shrug just wanna know what you're thinking
I wanna tell you but I can't so I lie
I can't tell you how being around you makes me
at peace
I can't tell you that every time you touch me I
feel at ease
Or everytime your arms are around me I feel
relieved
I can't let you know you're my everything
That would be foolish of me
I wish i could be honest
But i gotta stay guarded
If i could tell you the truth
Would you call me a fool
Because I'm madly in love with you
And there's not a single thing I can do
But I wouldn't dare because to be honest that
wouldn't be fair.

Truce

For so long I defended you
Because I saw past the dark
I kept loving you
Even after you broke my heart
Over and over you hurt me
You would stich me up
But I kept on bleeding
You'd kiss the wound
And promise me healing
But then turn around
Just to deceive me
Around and around
This vicious circle
That we called love
And maybe for a short while
It was
Or maybe I'm to fucked up
To even know
I wanted things to work
But the good can't outweigh the hurt
You're not good for me
Now All we have is our memories
And our beautiful daughter
I hope she gets to know her Father
We have our differences

And we both have our pain
But I'm tired of the who hurts more game
We both put each other through shit
But we're we're adults
And It's time we start acting like it

Beautiful Girl

Beautiful girl

With eyes that shine

You've been hurting

For quite some time

Beautiful girl

With fragile wings

She forgot the words

But still she sings

Beautiful girl

With a heavy heart

Her soul is bright

But remains in the dark

Beautiful girl

With a cracked soul

But even shattered pieces

Create a whole

Beautiful girl

With a touch so soft

A beautiful girl

Who is so lost

She wants to be free

Swimming in misery

Longing for peace

But Stuck in between

A beautiful girl

With a beautiful soul

Lives a life

In the freezing cold

Didn't Realize

Didn't realize

how broken I am inside

I try and hide

this pain in my eyes

But you can't run

from yourself

No matter how hard you try.

Never thought I'd become

something I despise.

I'd rather feel this hurt

than be numb

I guess it could be worse;

I could be lost in drugs

But that's what I do

I weigh out the bad

But it's not any better

if I'm lost in a tab

That's where you can go

if you really wanna know

At the end of a bottle

Drowning myself in liquor

Slowly going insane

I'm playing my cards right

but too lost in the game

Tables Have Turned

You hate me fore the shit you did

Baby I never wanted it to be like this

But you lied straight to my face

I ignored it and pushed through the pain

I gave you the benefit of the doubt

You betrayed me and now hate me

For what I'm all about

Telling me to come back to you

After the shit you put me through

Its like telling someone to walk it off

After boeing shot

You're still selfish

Maybe I'm in the wrong

And I know you're trying

But on my mind is still all the lying

All the nights you left me crying

The bad outweighs the good

No this isn't how it should be

But I don't know how to be happy

Baby I wish we could

I wish I would

But how is that fair

To tell me I don't care

When I gave you 4 years

And all I got were tears

Why baby tell me why

You can't see the pain in my eyes

While I stare At The Stars

I'm in a daze

So much in my head

Constantly dragging

I wanna be ahead

I feel stuck in a rut

The same every day

I know I'm on track

But it feels real delayed

I wanna do something

Feel like someone

Make a change

Become who I wanna become

I know I'll get there

It's just hard

So I'll just hope and pray

While I stare at the stars

Double Edged Sword

I know the darkness all to well
I have been here before
I told myself I wouldn't revisit
 I looked at myself and I swore
But here we are again
Crying over things I can't control
Gluing back all my pieces
Just so I can somewhat feel whole I am
beautifully broken
That is what I tell myself
But it's nothing but a lie
A lie I know to well
Fake it till you make it
Smile through the pain
But sometimes the tears
Have me bounded in chains
Fighting with myself everyday
I'm never prepared for battle
I suit up in my armor
But I am oh so very fragile
The worst part about the dark
Is knowing
I don't belong here
But I'm stuck in quick stand
And Fighting against fear

I have scars
I have wounds
I am a warrior
but feel so defeated
I'm using a double edged sword
 To fight off my demons

IDK

Falling back into toxic habits
Been having deja vu
Am I over thinking
Or is this gut feeling true
Anxiety screams
And intuition whispers
But my brain is always loud
And it's so fixed on her
I'm in over my head
Why can't it be easy
Why can't I be secure instead
You've gone out of your way
To make sure she's still there
Even if it means losing me
Am I being unfair
Do you even fucking care
Over and over I tell you how I feel
But you don't hear what I say
So I gotta turn the other cheek
And pretend that I'm okay
But I feel myself drifting
Further and further each day
And I don't know what more
You want me to say

My Mental

I am definitely broken
And fuxked up
The people before
Had me convinced
I'm not enough
I've always been
The one to love
But when will
It be my turn
I start the fire
And watch myself burn
I play with the matches
And wonder why I hurt
I'm sorry I question your love
But people before you
Have broken my trust
It shouldn't be such a fuss
But when you open up
A little piece is taken each time
And you gotta suck it up
And pretend your just fine
Even if you're compeltley breaking inside

Free Spirit

I wanna make out at red lights
And not stop until it turns green
I wanna speed down the highway
Make me feel like a teen
Roll down all the windows
And feel the wind in my hair
Let go of all my worries
For a little while just not care
I wanna feel alive
I wanna feel that rush
And maybe get a glimpse
of stupid young love

Waiting

Day by day I hope you say the words
Always waiting for what i wanna hear
That you want me
And it's ever so clear
I wait for the time it's easy
And it doesn't have to hurt
Where you choose me
And I don't have to worry
But that's just wishful thinking
Because the ship has already
Started sinking
And now I begin to sink in

Catastrophe

I've been running for so long
Trying to mask my pain
Don't know where I belong
Been trying so hard to remain sane
But am I really trying
When I have all these drugs going to my brain
Or is it all just an illusion
Been trying to figure out what's wrong
But haven't come to a conclusion
All these problems I'm trying to solve
It's the simplest of solutions
It involves heavy doses of pollution
I think I'm just being stupid
Oh God help me I feel so useless
Going about my life feeling so clueless
Why does life have to be so ruthless
I'm tired of being strong
I'm hearing the lyrics but not the song
Where in the fuck did i go wrong ?

My Love

I wish my heart wouldn't take the lead
Because now you mean the world to me
It wasn't my intention to fall
But with me it's everything or
Nothing at all
I've always worn my heart on my sleeve
And it's always gotten the best of me
To love deeply can be a curse
But not loving is so much worse
And it's an honor loving you
I wish you could see your worth
I hope you keep me around long enough to live
up to my word
I want to do what no one's ever done and put you
first
Give you what you deserve
Because no matter what you say
You deserve the fucking world